Judaism
in words and pictures

Sarah Thorley
Designed and illustrated by the author

CONTENTS

WORD LIST

Torah   the holy writings of the Jews, the first five books of the Bible
Talmud   the 'encyclopaedia' which explains and discusses the Torah
Israel   the Jewish State (this region has also been called Canaan, Judaea and Palestine)
Hebrew   the language spoken by the early Jews and in Israel today
Moses   the great leader through whom God gave the Torah to the Jews
the Covenant   agreement (or promise) made between God and Abraham
the Messiah   a leader awaited by Jews, in whose time God will bring justice and peace to the world
Shabbat (Sabbath)   the weekly day of rest, recreation and worship for Jews
synagogue   the building where Jews meet for worship, study and community events
rabbi   expert on and teacher of Torah and often leader of a synagogue
mitzvah   (plural mitzvot)   duty or 'good deed' to be done according to the command of God
Bar Mitzvah   means 'Son of the Commandment'. At the age of 13 a boy becomes Bar Mitzvah and begins to join in the adult activities of the Jewish community. This is marked by a special service in the synagogue.
Pesah (Passover)   the festival to celebrate the escape from slavery in Egypt
kosher   describes food which has been prepared according to Jewish laws
kiddush   blessing over wine to celebrate Shabbat and festivals
menorah   the seven-branched lamp that stood in the Temple. An important symbol of Judaism
tallit   a shawl worn by men when they pray
tefillin   small boxes containing Bible verses, which men tie to their arm and forehead for prayer
kippah (or kappel or yarmulkah)   the small cap worn by men
to fast   to go without food or drink for a certain time

Dates   B.C.E. stands for Before the Common Era (the time before Jesus was born). C.E. stands for Common Era (the time since the birth of Jesus). For Jewish dates see p.25.

1 Torah

Torah is the centre of the Jewish religion. It is the word of God.

The Hebrew word *torah* means 'law' or 'teaching', but it means much more than that to Jews. It means a way by which to live. Jews believe that the five books of the Torah contain the words that God spoke to Moses on Mount Sinai about 3400 years ago (see Chapters 2 and 6). God gave Moses wisdom and knowledge to guide his people in a godly way of life for all time. Jews have loved and studied the Torah and obeyed its teachings ever since.

The top photograph shows Jews dancing with the Torah at the joyful festival of Simhat Torah. The Torah is read aloud every week in the synagogue. During each year the whole of the Torah is read. Simhat Torah is held in the week when the end of the Torah is reached. The people dance around the synagogue and even into the street, carrying the Torah scrolls. Then the reading begins again from the first chapter.

These boys are learning how the scrolls should be read at a synagogue service. After the age of thirteen a boy may be called upon to read the Torah during a service. Notice the *yad*, the silver pointer, used to follow the words. The Torah is holy and the writing should not be touched by hand.

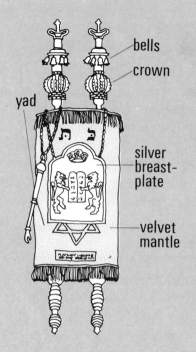

bells

crown

yad

silver breast-plate

velvet mantle

When not in use, scrolls are 'dressed' (like this) and kept in the Ark (the special cupboard in the synagogue, see p. 5). During a service the scrolls are taken out of the Ark and carried around the synagogue. The covers and ornaments are taken off for the readings. Children may be invited to 'dress' the scrolls again afterwards.

For use in the synagogue the Torah is always kept in the form of a scroll.

The photographs on this page show a Torah scroll being made. First the animal skin is prepared. Next the scribe carefully writes the whole Torah by hand with a quill pen. It will take him more than a year to write. Lastly the writings are sewn on to two wooden rollers.

The Torah is written in the Hebrew language. It is read from right to left (see p.14). The names of the five books of the Torah are: Genesis, Exodus, Leviticus, Numbers and Deuteronomy. They are the first five books of the Hebrew Bible. This Bible was written down over many hundreds of years. It contains the words God spoke to a number of holy men and tells how God acted in the lives of the Jewish people.

The Hebrew Bible contains history, laws, songs, poems, prophecy (telling God's will) and ethics (what is right and wrong). They are the same writings that Christians call the Old Testament in their Bible. So Christians and Jews share many of the same beliefs about God. Muslims also look on many of the people in the Bible as holy.

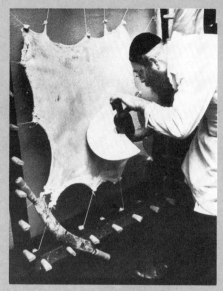

1. What was the name of the man to whom God spoke the words of the Torah?
2. What does the festival of Simhat Torah celebrate?
3. (a) Look at the photograph of Simhat Torah opposite. Can you write down at least three things the men and boys are doing? (b) Why do you think they are doing these things?
4. Look at the picture of the boys reading the scrolls. How can you tell that the boys are Jewish?
5. Why is one of the boys using a yad?
6. In the middle picture above, in what language is the scribe writing? Why?
7. The five books in the Torah are the same as the first five books in the Christian Bible. What are they called?
8. What things will you find in the Hebrew Bible?
9. Draw a scroll (a) open for reading and (b) 'dressed'. Label your drawings.

2 One God

This is the land where the Jewish religion began about 3800 years ago. In those days people worshipped many gods. A man named Abraham taught that there was only one *all*-mighty God who had created the world. People should worship only Him.

The Torah tells how God made a Covenant with Abraham. Abraham and his family would be the start of a special people. They would be God's 'chosen people' and He would be their God and give them a land of their own. God would speak to them and lead them so that they might show the rest of the world how great and good God is.

Judaism is a very old religion. Abraham lived about 1800 years before Christianity began and 2400 years before Islam began. The Christian and Islamic beliefs in one God came from the teaching of Abraham.

You can read about the first Jews in the Torah. One of Abraham's grandsons was called Jacob, or Israel, which is why his descendants are called *Israelites* or *Children of Israel*. Israel had twelve sons who each became father of a tribe. One of them was called Judah, which is where the word *Jew* comes from. Hebrew was the language of the early Jews, so Jews were sometimes called *Hebrews*.

About 400 years after Abraham the Israelites were slaves in Egypt. God chose Moses to lead them out of Egypt, across the Red Sea to freedom. This escape is known as the Exodus (see p. 22). The Israelites then spent many years in the Sinai Desert. Here the most important event in Jewish history took place. You can read in the Torah (Exodus, Chapters 19 and 20) how God spoke to Moses and repeated His Covenant with His people. God gave Moses the Torah, which describes how Jews should live. The Ten Commandments, written on tablets of stone (see p. 12), were part of that Law.
A symbol of these two tablets of stone is to be found in most synagogues (see pictures on pp. 5, 10, 11, 13, 28).

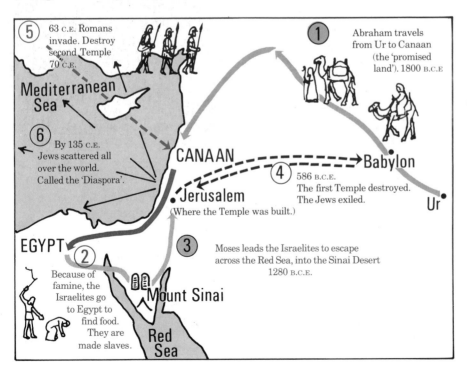

(5) 63 C.E. Romans invade. Destroy second Temple 70 C.E.

Mediterranean Sea

(6) By 135 C.E. Jews scattered all over the world. Called the 'Diaspora'.

CANAAN

Jerusalem
(Where the Temple was built.)

EGYPT

(2) Because of famine, the Israelites go to Egypt to find food. They are made slaves.

Mount Sinai

Red Sea

(3) Moses leads the Israelites to escape across the Red Sea, into the Sinai Desert 1280 B.C.E.

(4) 586 B.C.E. The first Temple destroyed. The Jews exiled.

Babylon

Ur

(1) Abraham travels from Ur to Canaan (the 'promised land'). 1800 B.C.E

The Israelites made an Ark in which to keep and carry the tablets of the Law, wherever they went. When at last they settled in Canaan (the land God had promised them) they built a holy Temple in the city of Jerusalem and placed the Ark in it. Today, in every synagogue, the Torah scrolls are kept in a special cupboard called the Ark. It is the holiest part of the synagogue and faces towards Jerusalem. This photograph was taken in a synagogue in Israel. The Ark is behind the velvet curtain. Notice the tablets of the Ten Commandments. The lions are the symbol of the tribe of Judah. The crown is a symbol of God as king of all creation. (See also drawing on p. 3.)

About 600 years after Moses, in 586 B.C.E., the Temple was destroyed and the Jews were exiled (sent away) to Babylon and other far-off places. Later some of them came back and built a new Temple. After nearly another 500 years the Jews came under Roman rule. It was during their rule that the Jew called Jesus of Nazareth lived. In 70 C.E. the Romans destroyed the second Temple and it has never been rebuilt. Again the Jews were scattered. For about 1900 years after that the Jews had no country of their own. Then in 1948, in the region that once was called Canaan, the State of Israel was set up (see Chapter 4).

On the right is the only part of the Temple which still stands. It is the Western Wall, sometimes called the 'Wall of Tears' or the 'Wailing Wall'. Jews from all over the world come here to pray. They pray for the rebuilding of the Temple and for the coming of the Messiah, as foretold in the Bible. The Messiah will be God's messenger who will bring justice and peace to the world and lead all people to believe in the one true God. Jews do not believe, as Christians do, that Jesus was that awaited Messiah.

1. Describe the picture of the land where the Jewish religion began. What kind of country does it look like?
2. What did Abraham teach?
3. (a) What is a covenant?   (b) What was God's Covenant with Abraham?
4. Look at the map. (a) Where did Abraham start and end his journey?   (b) Why did the Israelites go to Egypt?   (c) Who led the Israelites out of slavery in Egypt?   (d) What did they build in Jerusalem? (e) What happened in 70 C.E.?
5. In synagogues today the Torah scrolls are kept in a special cupboard. Why is it called the Ark?
6. Why do you think the Western Wall of the Temple in Jerusalem is called the Wall of Tears?
7. Draw a picture of an Ark in a synagogue. Show the symbols of the lions, the tablets of stone and the crown. (See also pictures on pp. 10 and 13.)

3 Jews today

Today there are Jews living in most countries in the world. There are more Jews (about five million) in the U.S.A. than anywhere else. The second largest number of Jews are now in Israel (about three and a half million).

BRITISH JEWS
There are 56 million people in Britain; about one-third of a million are Jewish. There have been Jews living in Britain since the Norman Conquest in 1066. Sometimes it has been a good and safe place for Jews, at other times they have been badly treated and even expelled. In the last hundred years or so, Jews have become leaders in many fields. The photographs below show some well-known Jews of today.

ROSE HEILBRON First woman Judge ▼

STUART YOUNG Head of the BBC ▼

◄ MARJORIE PROOPS Journalist

Marks & Spencer was started in 1884 in Leed by Simon Marks, a poor Jewish immigran

MARKS' PENNY BAZAAR

▲ YEHUDI MENUHIN Violinist

▲ GERALD KAUFMAN Politician

Jews have lived through some very terrible times. Perhaps the most terrible was only fifty years ago. During the Second World War six million Jews were beaten, starved or gassed to death by the German Nazis, just because they were Jews. In the picture on the left elderly women and children are being pushed into cattle trucks which will take them to the death camps. Notice the yellow stars that Jews were forced to wear. Most Jews you meet today will have had relatives who died in the Holocaust, as it is called.

The notice-board below is in London. The swastika 卍 was the sign of the Nazi party, whose members hated Jews. It is still sometimes used by evil or ignorant people who hate other people because they are different in some way. ('Juden raus' means 'Jews get out'.)

There are Jews of many nationalities: French, American, African, Russian, etc. There are also Orthodox, Hasidic and Progressive Jews. These are the names of different branches of the Jewish faith. (You may also hear of Reform, Liberal and Conservative Jews. These are similar to the Progressive Jews.)

ORTHODOX JEWS have been the mainstream of Judaism since early times. They hold strictly to God's law as given to Moses in the Torah. Most of the pictures in this book are of Orthodox Jews.

HASIDIC JEWS come mainly from the towns in Eastern Europe. During the Middle Ages in Europe there were times when Jews were forced to live in separate districts, called *ghettos*. In spite of much poverty and hardship, many of these communities flourished. They were led by wise and holy men called *rebbes*. They set up their own hospitals, shops, schools and religious law courts. These were the Hasidic Jews. There are Hasidic Jews in most parts of the world today, but they still mix mainly with each other. They speak their own language called Yiddish. They will not allow anything modern to change their religious customs. You can recognize them by their dress. Below is a street party at the festival of Succot (see p. 27) in London. A long black coat, large fur hat and a beard are worn by many of the men. Boys have short hair with long sidelocks.

PROGRESSIVE JEWS

In Western Europe after about 1800 it became possible for Jews to mix much more freely with the citizens of their country. At last they could join in with university, business and political life. Some of these Jews, and others who had settled in America, wanted to make their religious ideas and practices more modern. They started Progressive branches of Judaism. In the synagogue they began to read the Torah in modern languages and they allowed men and women to sit together. Women could now become rabbis (like the one below) and families no longer kept all the strict kosher food laws (see p. 16). Orthodox Jews are not happy about these changes so there is some bad feeling between these groups.

1. For about how many years have there been Jews living in Britain?
2. How and where did Marks & Spencer begin?
3. What is happening to the women and children in the picture on p. 6?
4. Look again at the faces in that picture. How do you think the people are feeling?
5. What has been painted over the synagogue notice-board?
6. What was a ghetto?
7. Look at the photograph of the London street party above. How would you know the people are Hasidic Jews?
8. Write down two of the practices which make Progressive Jews different from Orthodox Jews.
9. Imagine you are one of the children at the street party above. Write a paragraph about what you did when you got up that morning.

4 Israel

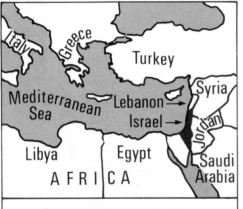

Israel is only a little larger than Wales. You could drive from north to south in about 10 hours. About 4 million people live there. Nearly 3½ million are Jews.

This is Jerusalem, the capital city of Israel. The Temple of the Jews once stood here. Now all that is left is part of the Western Wall (in the middle of the picture). There are always Jews praying at this spot. Boys come here for their Bar Mitzvah, great crowds gather at festivals (see pp. 5, 23 and 27 for more pictures). You can see the spires of Christian churches and the domes of Muslim mosques. Jerusalem has become a very holy place for Christians and Muslims also. Look at the street name on the left.

This map shows you where Israel is. Nearly a quarter of the Jews in the world live there now. The first Israelites arrived there nearly 4000 years ago (see Chapter 2). Since then this small land has been conquered and lived in and ruled by many nations: Philistines, Greeks, Syrians, Romans, Crusaders, Arabs, Turks.... For a short time, forty years ago, it was even under British rule. There have always been some Jews living there. Other Jews, scattered around the world, have dreamed of going back to their 'promised land'. 'Next year in Jerusalem' are the hopeful words said after the Pesah meal every year (see p. 22).

About 100 years ago the Zionist movement began to plan for Jews to return to the land of Israel. (Zion is another name for Israel.) Gradually Jews began to go back and buy land from the Arabs or the Turks and settle down. In the picture on the left they are fixing up a water-pumping station in the desert so they can start farming. It was not until 1948, after the Second World War, that the State of Israel was set up. Six million Jews had been killed by the Nazis, thousands more Jews were left with no homes. Many nations supported the Jews in their desire to have their own homeland where they could live in safety. So now Israel is governed by Jews and supported by other Jews from all over the world. But there is still conflict because the Arabs who were already there did not want the Jews to come. Ever since then the Arabs and the Jews have been fighting each other, as you can see in the middle picture opposite. It is hard to know what is right. The hope is that one day they will live and work together in peace. The lower picture opposite shows an Arab and a Jew talking together in the streets of Jerusalem.

The photograph below was taken on a kibbutz. The first kibbutzim (plural) were started by groups of Jews about eighty years ago. They worked together to make poor land into rich farmland. Now there are about 250 kibbutzim in Israel. A kibbutz is a place where a group of families live together. They share all the work and the money they make. Their children all play and learn together and all the members decide together how their lives should be run. Below families are preparing the *huppah* (see p. 20) for a wedding on the kibbutz.

1. What can you see in the photograph of Jerusalem above?
2. For which three religions is Jerusalem a holy city?
3. What are the three languages on the street sign opposite? Which goes with which religion?
4. What is the man doing in the photograph at the bottom of p. 8?
5. When was the State of Israel set up?
6. Why is there fighting between Arabs and Jews in Israel?
7. Look at the photograph of the Arab and the Jew talking. How can you tell which is which?
8. What is a kibbutz? Would you like to live on a kibbutz?
9. What is happening in the kibbutz photograph above?
10. Draw a map to show where Israel is.

5 Synagogues

A synagogue is a building where Jews go to worship, to meet each other, to study and to ask advice on religious matters. On the right is a synagogue in Israel.

The main service is held each week on Saturday (Shabbat).

The middle photograph shows Jews at worship in London in an Orthodox synagogue. Men and married women cover their heads. Men put on a tallit (prayer shawl) when they pray. Men and women do not sit together.
The service is nearly all in Hebrew. It is often led by a cantor who has been trained to chant the words. The rabbi usually gives the sermon (the teaching part). The most important moment in the service is when the Torah is read. The scrolls are taken out of the Ark to the bimah (see picture opposite). Between three and seven men may have the honour of being called up to read. (See also Chapter 1.)

The bottom picture shows Progressive Jews (see p. 7). The Ark is open ready for the scrolls to be lifted out. Notice that women are taking part in the service and they are sitting with the men. This would not happen in an Orthodox synagogue. Another main difference is that only part of the service is in Hebrew, the rest is in English.

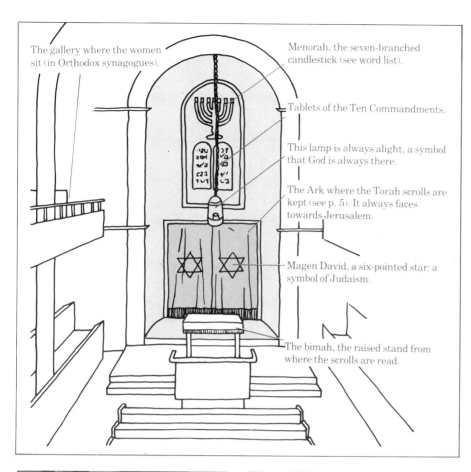

The gallery where the women sit (in Orthodox synagogues).

Menorah, the seven-branched candlestick (see word list).

Tablets of the Ten Commandments.

This lamp is always alight, a symbol that God is always there.

The Ark where the Torah scrolls are kept (see p. 5). It always faces towards Jerusalem.

Magen David, a six-pointed star: a symbol of Judaism.

The bimah, the raised stand from where the scrolls are read.

In many synagogues, members pay a yearly rent for a seat. This is one of the ways a synagogue raises the money it needs. Money is never collected during a service. The picture above shows a man's seat under which he keeps his tallit, his siddur and his tefillin (see p. 17). The siddur is the prayer book with the words of the services in it.

After the Shabbat service there is often a *kiddush* (a blessing over a cup of wine), particularly if there is a special event which a family wants to share with the rest of the people.

A nursery school meets in this synagogue hall during the week. These children are learning about what happens at a synagogue service. They will learn about Jewish history and festivals too.

Most synagogues have a 'Ladies Guild'. Its members meet often to plan parties and other events and to raise money. These two ladies are getting ready a meal in the synagogue hall.

1. What is a synagogue for?
2. How can you tell that the building at the top of p. 10 is a synagogue? (There are at least three clues.)
3. On which day is the main service held each week?
4. What is the most important part of the Shabbat service?
5. Look at the photographs of the two services shown opposite. How can you tell which is Orthodox and which is Progressive?
6. What can you see under the seat lid in the photograph at the top of this page?
7. Choose one of the three photographs above and explain everything you can see in it.
8. Write down some of the differences between a synagogue and a church (or another place of worship that you know).
9. Copy the drawing of the synagogue above. Put in the labels.

6 Mitzvot

After the escape from Egypt, the Israelites travelled on until they came to the desert of Sinai. God said to Moses, 'If you will obey me and keep your Covenant with me, then you shall be my chosen people.' There was thunder and lightning and a thick cloud lay upon Mount Sinai. Moses led the people to the foot of the mountain then went alone up into the cloud and God spoke to him for a long time. When he came down, Moses had two tablets of stone carved with these words of God:

1. I alone am your God.
2. You shall worship no other God.
3. Do not dishonour my name (e.g. swear using God's name).
4. Remember the Sabbath day and keep it holy.
5. Respect your father and your mother.
6. Do not murder.
7. Do not steal.
8. Do not commit adultery (be unfaithful to your wife or husband).
9. Do not tell lies about anyone.
10. Do not envy (want) what belongs to someone else.

This, in modern words, is what the Torah says in Exodus, Chapters 19 and 20. These are the Ten Commandments which every Jew tries to obey. They were given about 3400 years ago. Are they still good rules for life today?

Are you wondering why this page is headed Mitzvot? Mitzvah means 'a command of God' (mitzvot is the plural). The Ten Commandments are the best known, but many more mitzvot are listed in the Torah. To do good deeds for God and for other people – to perform mitzvot – is a very important part of the Jewish religion. The pictures on this van show some of the most important mitzvot. (See p. 17 for tefillin and mezuzah.) Lubavitch is the name of a group of Hasidic Jews.

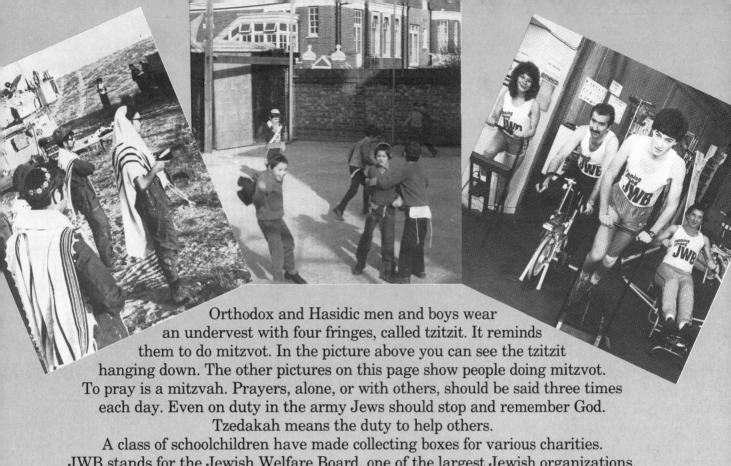

Orthodox and Hasidic men and boys wear
an undervest with four fringes, called tzitzit. It reminds
them to do mitzvot. In the picture above you can see the tzitzit
hanging down. The other pictures on this page show people doing mitzvot.
To pray is a mitzvah. Prayers, alone, or with others, should be said three times
each day. Even on duty in the army Jews should stop and remember God.
Tzedakah means the duty to help others.
A class of schoolchildren have made collecting boxes for various charities.
JWB stands for the Jewish Welfare Board, one of the largest Jewish organizations.
Young Jews are training for the London Marathon to raise money for blind and disabled people.
Children are bringing gifts to old people at the festival of Hannukah (see p. 26).
Preparing the synagogue room for a service is a mitzvah
for an elderly man at a home for the aged.

Note   You will need a Bible.
1.   What was Moses carrying when he came down from Mount Sinai?
2.   Is there a day in your week which is set aside for worship of God? If so, which day is it?
3.   Think about the Ten Commandments, one by one. Are they all good rules for life today?
4.   What does 'mitzvot' mean?
5.   Write down five of the mitzvot shown on the side of the Lubavitch van.
6.   (a) Which pictures on this page show mitzvot to help other people?
     (b) Which pictures on this page show duty towards God?
7.   Read Exodus, Chapters 19 and 20. Look at the photograph of Mount Sinai opposite. Imagine you were there. Write
     a story saying what you saw and how you felt about it. Illustrate it, if you like.

7 Study

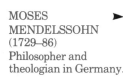

◄ MOSES MAIMONIDES
(1135–1204)
Thinker, writer and
doctor in Spain.

MOSES
MENDELSSOHN ►
(1729–86)
Philosopher and
theologian in Germany.

◄ BARON LIONEL
DE ROTHSCHILD
(1808–79)
The Rothschild family
have been famous
bankers in Europe for
nearly 200 years. ►

ALBERT EINSTEIN
(1879–1955)
Brilliant scientist,
famous for his
'Theory of Relativity'.

Books and learning have always been very important to Jews. For example, from 900 to 1200 Spain, though ruled by Muslims, was a great centre of Jewish religion and learning. There were many famous Jewish writers, poets, thinkers and scientists during that 'Golden Age' as it is now known. Even in the ghettos (see p. 7), when Jews were not allowed to join in everyday life around them, they found comfort and joy in studying together. Look at the pictures of four famous Jews on the right.

Today, young Jewish children listen to the Bible stories about great heroes like Moses, David, Daniel, Ruth and Esther. They learn to join in the prayers at home. The table mat on the right shows you one of the first prayers a child learns.

Here is the Hebrew alphabet. Hebrew is read from right to left. At five or six years old Jewish children start to learn Hebrew. Some are taught by their parents, some go to *heder*. Heder or 'religion school' is a special class held in the synagogue, usually on Sundays. The children also learn about Jewish history. In many countries there are Jewish schools.

The photograph on the right was taken in a Jewish primary school in London.

The photograph above shows Jewish schoolboys learning to put on the tefillin for prayer (see p. 17). When he is thirteen a Jewish boy becomes Bar Mitzvah; a girl may become Bat Mitzvah (see p. 21). Boys have begun to study the Talmud, the 'encyclopaedia' that explains and discusses the Torah. Rabbis through the ages tried to answer questions about the Torah for the everyday needs of the people of their time. Their writings make up the Talmud. It was put together about 1500 years ago. It has 63 volumes and more than two-and-a-half million words. You can see why it is sometimes called 'the sea of learning'!

Many boys, and some girls, will go on to a *yeshiva* when they are about eighteen. A yeshiva is a college for the study of the Torah and the Talmud. Yeshiva students, like the ones in this picture taken in Israel, may spend one year or as many as twenty years studying. Some may then become teachers or rabbis.

RABBIS

Rabbis spend much of their lives studying. A rabbi's most important work is to teach God's laws and message from the Torah. He also encourages and helps people and gives advice about what is right and wrong. He preaches in the synagogue and visits the sick. Many rabbis are leaders of a synagogue. Most rabbis are married. Orthodox Jews have only men rabbis. Progressive Jews have women rabbis also.

These two young men are training to become rabbis in a Jewish college in London.

These rabbis are visiting a day centre for elderly and blind people.

1. What was the Golden Age in Spain?
2. What words can you read on Matthew's place mat?
3. How can you tell that the photograph opposite was taken in a *Jewish* primary school?
4. What do young children do at heder?
5. What is the Talmud?
6. Why is the Talmud sometimes called 'the sea of learning'?
7. (a) What is a rabbi's most important work?   (b) What other things does a rabbi do?
8. What can you see in the picture of the rabbis visiting a day centre?
9. Copy the Hebrew letters tav, vav, resh and hay. You will have written the word 'Torah'. (Remember to write the letters from right to left.)

8 In a Jewish home

mezuzah

The home, even more than the synagogue, has always been the centre of Jewish life and religion. These two pages show how God is remembered all the time in a Jewish home.

The picture on the left shows a mezuzah. You will see one on the right front doorpost of most Jewish homes. Often one is fixed to each doorpost inside the house as well. It is a small case, inside which are verses from the Torah called the *shema*. A mezuzah shows that God is present in this house and that this family keeps God's laws.

These are the words of the shema (in English):
'Hear, O Israel, the Lord our God is one. Love the Lord your God with all your heart, with all your soul, and with all your strength. Never forget these commands ... Teach them to your children. Repeat them when you are at home and when you are away ... Tie them on your arm and wear them on your forehead as a reminder. Write them on the doorposts of your house.'
Deuteronomy 6: 4–9.

A KOSHER KITCHEN

1 Soak for half an hour in water,
2 sprinkle with salt.
3 After one hour rinse meat.

= for milk products

= for meat products

Koshering meat

This kosher kitchen has two separate sinks, drawers and cupboards. This is because different pots, pans, plates and cutlery should be used for meat and for milk dishes.

Kosher and non-kosher

Animals must have cloven hooves and chew the cud.

Poultry may be eaten but not birds of prey.

Fish must have fins and scales and a backbone.

The food eaten by Jews should be *kosher* food. Kosher means allowed. Food which is not allowed is listed in the Bible in Leviticus, Chapter 11. All meat must be koshered: that is, the animal must be killed swiftly and without pain with a knife, and the blood drained away. It must then be prepared as shown in the drawing above. Meat and milk foods should not be eaten at the same meal. These kosher laws are kept more strictly by some Jews than by others. It is best to ask, if you are inviting a Jew to a meal.

Jews try to keep close links with all members of their family. Grandparents, children, in-laws, uncles and aunts gather together for special occasions, for festivals and often for Shabbat. Nor should visitors or strangers be left out. It is a mitzvah to welcome any visitor into your home.

The Fifth Commandment says: 'Honour your father and your mother....' Sons learn about Torah and prayer from their fathers. Daughters learn from their mothers how to keep a kosher home. In times when synagogues were destroyed and Jews were not allowed to meet together for worship, no one could stop the Jewish faith living on in the home.

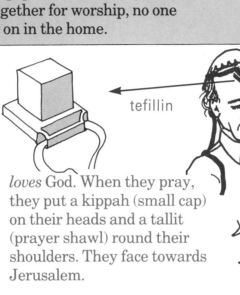

tallit

tefillin

Prayers are said three times a day and before and after meals. This Orthodox Jew is helping his son put on the *tefillin* before they pray. Tefillin are small leather boxes with Bible writings in them. One is fastened round the boy's head to show that he *thinks* about God. The other is fastened to his left arm, near to his heart, to show that he *loves* God. When they pray, they put a kippah (small cap) on their heads and a tallit (prayer shawl) round their shoulders. They face towards Jerusalem.

The Shabbat meal is prepared at a Jewish home for the elderly.

Jews buy their meat from special kosher butchers.

1. What is a mezuzah?
2. What are the commands in the shema which a Jew must never forget?
3. Why are tefillin fixed to the forehead and to the left arm?
4. What is the Fifth Commandment?
5. What does kosher food mean?
6. What words are over the serving hatches in the photograph above? Why?
7. If you had Jewish friends to a meal, which of these things would you *not* give them to eat?
   Bacon, bread, chicken, prawns, cod, pork sausages, eel, beefburger.
8. Make a diagram to show how meat is koshered *or* draw a kippah and a tallit.

9 Shabbat

The Fourth Commandment says: 'Remember the Sabbath Day and keep it holy. Six days you shall work and the seventh day is the Sabbath of the Lord your God. You shall not do any work, neither you, nor your children, nor your servants. For in six days the Lord made heaven, the earth, the sea and all that is in them; therefore the Lord blessed the seventh day and made it holy.'

So Jews stop work one day every week to remember and to thank God for making the world. Indeed, the rest of the world got the idea of a day off each week from this Jewish law.

For most Jews, keeping Shabbat is one of the most important and joyful parts of their religion. This day is different from every other day of the week. It is for families to be together and to think about God.

It is Friday and the children below are learning how to make *hallah*, the special plaited bread eaten on Shabbat. Friday is a busy day. The house must be cleaned, all the food must be cooked and all the jobs finished before sunset. At sunset Shabbat begins; no more work will be done until sunset the next day.

'Shabbat shalom' (a peaceful Sabbath to you): this is the greeting for Shabbat. The sun has set; the men have gone off to synagogue for prayers. When they return they will find the table laid with the best white cloth, the two Shabbat candlesticks, a glass of wine at each place and a plate with the hallah covered by a special cloth. At sunset the mother lit the candles and welcomed in Shabbat with a prayer.

Now the father blesses the children and says kiddush. Kiddush is the prayer of blessing over the wine: 'Blessed art thou, O Lord our God, King of the Universe who creates the fruit of the vine....' Next the hallah is blessed and everyone eats a piece. Then the meal can begin. Sometimes they sing Shabbat songs. Often there are guests; no Jew should be left on his own for the Shabbat meal.

18

TIMES FOR THE PROVINCES							
SUNSET TIMES The beginning of Sabbaths and Festivals should not be later than 14 minutes before sunset.				TERMINATION TIMES FOR THE SABBATHS			
Belfast	Birmingham	Bournemouth	Leeds	Belfast	Birmingham	Bournemouth	
July 10	9.58	9.28	9.19	9.34	11.19	10.40	10.24	1(
20	9.46	9.18	9.10	9.23	11.01	10.25	10.11	1(
30	9.30	9.04	8.56	9.08	10.38	10.06	9.55	1(
Aug. 9	9.10	8.46	8.39	8.49	10.13	9.44	9.35	(
19	8.49	8.26	8.20	8.28	9.48	9.21	9.13	(
29	8.26	8.04	8.00	8.05	9.21	8.57	8.49	8
Sept. 8	8.01	7.41	7.38	7.41	8.54	8.32	8.25	8
18	7.35	7.17	7.16	7.16	8.27	8.06	8.01	8
28	7.10	6.53	6.53	6.51	8.01	7.42	7.39	7
Oct. 8	6.44	6.30	6.31	6.27	7.36	7.19	7.17	7
18	6.21	6.07	6.10	6.03	7.13	6.56	6.57	(
28	5.58	5.47	5.51	5.42	6.51	6.38	6.38	(
Nov. 7	5.38	5.28	5.33	5.22	6.33	6.20	6.23	(
17	5.20	5.12	5.19	5.05	6.17	6.06	6.10	(
27	5.08	5.01	5.08	4.53	6.08	5.57	6.01	5
Dec. 7	4.59	4.54	5.02	4.46	6.01	5.52	5.57	5
17	4.59	4.52	5.02	4.46	6.01	5.52	5.58	

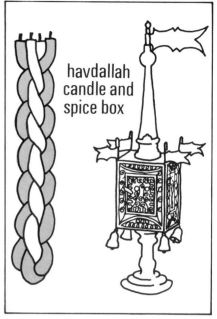

havdallah candle and spice box

The next morning the family goes to the synagogue service. After the midday meal (cooked the day before, of course), the time may be spent visiting friends, going for a walk, playing games, studying the Torah or just resting.

The photograph above was taken on a Shabbat in Israel. Notice there are no cars moving in the street. Many Jews try to live near enough to a synagogue to be able to walk there. On Shabbat strict Jews will not use any machines: no cars or buses, no telephone or television. These all need people to work them and Shabbat should be a day of complete rest for everyone (except, of course, if someone is ill or in danger). Sometimes it is difficult for Jews in Britain to get the day off work on Saturdays.

Above is part of a page from a Jewish pocket diary.

Shabbat ends with *Havdallah*, which means separation. It separates Shabbat from the rest of the week. At sunset on Saturday a blessing is said again over wine. A special plaited candle is lit. A box full of spices is passed around for all to smell, to carry the sweet smell of Shabbat into the coming week. The candle flame goes out as it is dipped in the wine and everyone wishes each other a good week.

A recipe for hallah

about 300 ml lukewarm water
1 level tbsp. dried yeast
1 tsp. sugar
½ kg flour
1 tsp. salt
1 tbsp. oil
1 egg and 1 yolk
poppy seeds

Stir yeast and sugar into a little of the water. Leave for 5 min. Sieve flour and salt into a bowl, make a well in the middle and put in egg, oil, yeast mixture and some of the water. Mix, adding more water if necessary, until bowl is clean. Knead on floured board until dough is smooth. Put in bowl, brush top with oil, cover with damp cloth and put in warm place for 1 hour. Push dough down into bowl, cover and leave to rise again. Divide dough into three pieces and roll into short strips. Plait and put on baking tray. Cover and leave to rise again. Brush with egg yolk and scatter on poppy seeds. Cook about 50 min. at Mark 5 or 190°C.

1. Why is Shabbat different from every other day of the week for Jews?
2. What is hallah?
3. Why is Friday a busy day for a Jewish mother?
4. What is the Shabbat greeting?
5. What is kiddush?
6. What does the page from the pocket diary show?
7. At what times did Shabbat begin and end on 29 and 30 August in Belfast?
8. Draw the havdallah candle and spice box.
9. Write about the large picture on the page opposite. What are the people doing? What can you see on the table? Look also at the Shabbat photograph on p. 17.

10 Family events

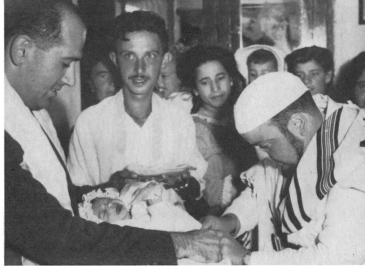

MARRIAGE

Jewish parents hope that their children will marry Jews so that the religion and customs will be carried on in their homes.

At a Jewish wedding the bride and bridegroom stand under a *huppah* (canopy). It is a symbol of the home they will make together. You can see the huppah clearly in the photograph on p. 9.

The bridegroom gives the bride a plain gold ring. Then the marriage agreement, called the *ketubah*, is read out. This contains the promises that the groom makes to the bride.

A blessing is said over two glasses of wine which the couple drink. Then – crack! – the groom crushes a glass under his foot. This is to show that life is not always easy; they must stay together through the bad as well as the good times and they must remember others who are not happy. As the couple step out from under the huppah, everyone calls 'Mazel Tov' (good luck), then a party is usually held.

The wedding card above shows a beautiful old ketubah.

A NEW BABY

Jewish babies are given a Hebrew name as well as an ordinary name. The Hebrew name is used in the synagogue and on religious documents such as the ketubah. A girl child is given her names and a blessing at the synagogue on the Shabbat after her birth.

A boy child is given his names at a ceremony of circumcision eight days after he is born. The family and close relatives gather together, usually at home, to rejoice. The foreskin of the baby's penis is cut off by a *mohel* (a Jew especially trained in this skill).

Jewish boys are circumcised because of the Covenant made between God and Abraham 3800 years ago, when God said: 'This is my Covenant which you shall keep, between me and you and your children after you. Every male shall be circumcised.' (Genesis 17: 10–14.)

BAR MITZVAH

On the Shabbat after his thirteenth birthday, a Jewish boy has his Bar Mitzvah ceremony. By then he has learned to read Hebrew well. For the first time he will be called up to read part of the Torah in front of everyone in the synagogue. This is a very proud moment for him and his family. Now he is grown up enough to keep all the Jewish laws and to be counted among the men of the congregation. The boy below is rehearsing his Torah reading before the service.

Nowadays many Jewish girls have a similar celebration, called a Bat Mitzvah. Bar Mitzvah means Son of the Commandment. Bat means daughter.

DEATH

The last words a Jew will say (if he can) are, 'Hear, O Israel, the Lord our God is one'. A day or two later, the body will be buried, in a plain wooden coffin, the head pointing towards Jerusalem. Prayers are said at the graveside. Orthodox Jews are always buried. Progressive Jews are sometimes cremated (burned). For the next seven days the family stay at home, sitting on low stools for much of the time and friends and relatives come to comfort them. Services may be held in the house once or twice a day. For the next three weeks life is very quiet, then it begins to return to normal. The children of the dead person say the *kaddish* prayer in the synagogue every week for eleven months. Every year, on the anniversary of her husband's death, the lady in the picture below lights a *Jahrzeit* candle and she and her children say the kaddish prayer.

1. What is a huppah? What does it symbolize?
2. What is the rabbi reading out at the wedding in the picture opposite?
3. Give one reason why the bridegroom crushes a glass under his foot.
4. Can you think of some Hebrew names (that is, names of people in the Hebrew Bible)?
5. Why are Jewish boys circumcised?
6. What is the boy doing in the photograph above?
7. How can you tell that the gravestones in the photograph above are in a Jewish cemetery?
8. In what way are people who have died remembered by their family on the anniversary of their death?
9. Design a wedding or a Bar Mitzvah card.

11 Pesah

'Why is this night different from all other nights?' asks the youngest member of the family at the Pesah seder every year. (Pesah is the Hebrew word for Passover.) In answer to that and three more questions, the story of 3400 years ago is told.

Seder is the meal and the service which take place on the first evening of the seven or eight days of Pesah. On the page opposite is a diagram of a table laid for the seder. Each thing on the table is a reminder of the story of the Exodus told in the Torah (Exodus, Chapters 12–14). It goes like this. The Israelites had been slaves in Egypt for 210 years. God promised Moses that He would help them escape to freedom. On a certain night the eldest son of every family in Egypt would die. The Israelites must mark their doorposts with the blood of a lamb. The angel of death would 'pass over' their houses and kill only the Egyptian boys. They must roast the lamb and eat it with bitter herbs and unleavened bread. (Unleavened means made without yeast: there would be no time to wait for bread with yeast to rise.) The Israelites did all these things and they left early the next morning. Moses led them as far as the Red Sea. They could not get across. They were trapped. Suddenly there was a strong wind and the waters parted. The Israelites passed safely through but the Egyptian soldiers who were chasing them were drowned when great waves crashed down on them.

God said to the Israelites: 'Keep this festival, for all time to come, because it was on this day that I brought you out of Egypt.'

Pesah takes place in the spring. The exact date changes each year according to the moon. Every Jewish home is spring-cleaned ready for this oldest and most famous Jewish festival. Pesah combines memories of suffering and of the joy of freedom. It also expresses the certainty of God's love for His people in times of trouble, both then and now.

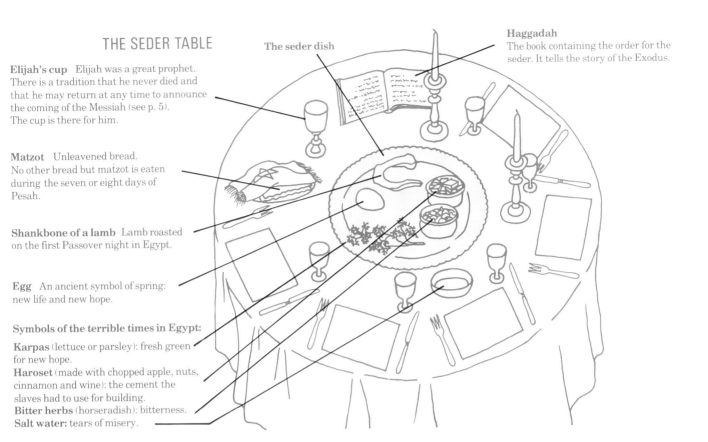

THE SEDER TABLE

The seder dish

Haggadah The book containing the order for the seder. It tells the story of the Exodus.

Elijah's cup Elijah was a great prophet. There is a tradition that he never died and that he may return at any time to announce the coming of the Messiah (see p. 5). The cup is there for him.

Matzot Unleavened bread. No other bread but matzot is eaten during the seven or eight days of Pesah.

Shankbone of a lamb Lamb roasted on the first Passover night in Egypt.

Egg An ancient symbol of spring: new life and new hope.

Symbols of the terrible times in Egypt:

Karpas (lettuce or parsley): fresh green for new hope.
Haroset (made with chopped apple, nuts, cinnamon and wine): the cement the slaves had to use for building.
Bitter herbs (horseradish): bitterness.
Salt water: tears of misery.

After Pesah comes the 'counting'. Seven weeks are counted, then the festival of Shavuot (also called Pentecost or the Festival of Weeks) is held. It celebrates the giving of the Law at Mount Sinai (see p. 12) seven weeks after the escape from Egypt.

It is also the beginning of harvest in Israel so the synagogues are decorated with flowers. The scrolls are dressed with wreaths and the Ten Commandments are read. These children are at the Western Wall in Jerusalem.

1. What is the boy doing in the photograph opposite?
2. What is a seder?
3. Why is the festival called Pesah or Passover?
4. What did God say to the Israelites after they had escaped?
5. What does the festival of Shavuot celebrate?
6. In the photograph above, what are the children carrying? Why do you think they have wreaths on their heads?
7. Draw a diagram of the seder dish and label the five things on it.
8. Write a story, imagining you were ten years old at the time of the Exodus. What did you see your parents doing that night? How did you help? What happened the next day? Were you afraid? Tired? Excited? What did you see? Read about it in the Bible.

12 The Jewish year

ROSH HASHANAH   The *shofar* (a ram's horn) has been sounding in the synagogue every day for a month. It calls Jews to the most serious festival of all: Rosh Hashanah, the Jewish New Year. In biblical times the shofar was often blown at important events and it has become a symbol for Jews. Rosh Hashanah begins in the Hebrew month of Tishri, in September or October. Jews send cards to each other. Another custom is to dip apples and hallah (bread) into honey as a symbol of hope that the New Year will be a sweet and happy one.

But this is also a solemn religious festival. It celebrates the creation of the world and it is a time when Jews think very hard about their lives and the wrongs they have done. Look at the picture below of a synagogue window in Birmingham. There is a tradition that at Rosh Hashanah God opens His 'Book of Life' in which everyone's name is written. God weighs up the good and the bad deeds each person has done over the past year. Can you see the judgement scales? (It is interesting that the zodiac sign for this time of year – Tishri – is a pair of weighing scales!)

On Rosh Hashanah afternoon many Jews go to the nearest river or beach and throw crumbs into the water. This action is called *tashlich*, it represents the throwing away of sins. The men below are on a beach in Israel. During the next ten days every Jew tries to say sorry to anyone to whom he has done wrong.

YOM KIPPUR
Then comes Yom Kippur, the Day of Atonement (which means making up for the wrong you have done), the day when God judges whether people are truly sorry for their wrongs. The synagogues are full all day long. People have come to ask God's forgiveness. Everyone, except those who are ill or under thirteen, fasts for twenty-five hours. That means they have no food or drink. This helps them to concentrate on God, to be sorry for their sins and to remember the hungry people in the world.

On the right is part of a page from an English/Hebrew pocket diary. At the top left it says JUNE 1986; at the top right it says SIVAN 5746. Sivan is the name of a Hebrew month; 5746 is the Jewish year. The Jews count their years from the creation of the world as told in the Bible. So it is 5746 years since then. (1986 is the number of years since Jesus was born. Christian countries count their years from that event.)

The diagram below shows the Jewish year with the Hebrew months. It also shows when the festivals occur and which part of the Torah is being read each month.

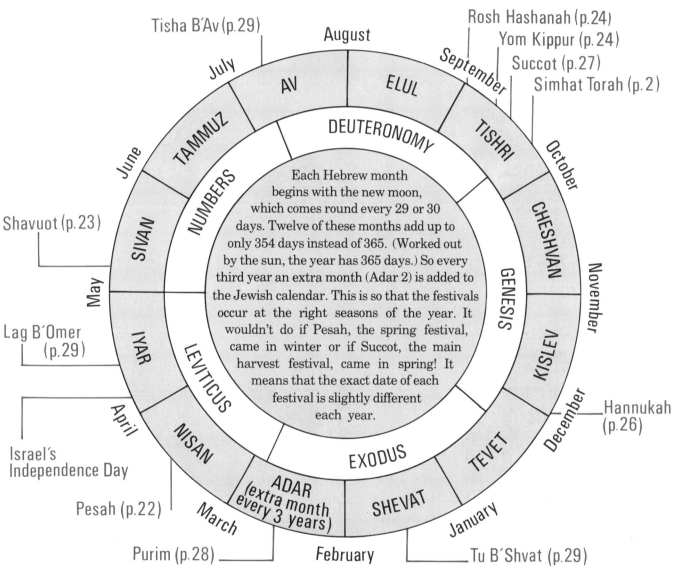

Each Hebrew month begins with the new moon, which comes round every 29 or 30 days. Twelve of these months add up to only 354 days instead of 365. (Worked out by the sun, the year has 365 days.) So every third year an extra month (Adar 2) is added to the Jewish calendar. This is so that the festivals occur at the right seasons of the year. It wouldn't do if Pesah, the spring festival, came in winter or if Succot, the main harvest festival, came in spring! It means that the exact date of each festival is slightly different each year.

1. Look at the man wearing the tallit, opposite. What is he doing?
2. What does the festival of Rosh Hashanah celebrate?
3. In the picture opposite, why are the five men on the beach?
4. What does every Jew try to do during the ten days between Rosh Hashanah and Yom Kippur?
5. What do Jews do on the day of Yom Kippur?
6. Which book of the Torah is read during the month of Shevat?
7. Which festivals are celebrated during the month of Tishri?
8. In which Hebrew month is Hannukah? What is the Christian month at that time?
9. Look carefully at the synagogue window opposite. Draw the four small pictures which show symbols for Rosh Hashanah and Yom Kippur and write down what they are.

13 Hannukah and Succot

HANNUKAH (also called the Festival of Lights)

In December if you see a candlestick like the one above burning in a window, you will know this is a Jewish home and that it is the festival of Hannukah.

In 175 B.C.E. the Syrian ruler Antiochus tried to destroy Judaism. He took over the holy Temple in Jerusalem. After ten years of fighting, a brave band of Jews led by Judah Maccabee defeated the Syrian armies and won back the Temple. They lit the Temple lamp (called a menorah) once again but there was only enough specially prepared oil for it to burn for one day. By a miracle it burned for eight days until some more oil was ready.

The Hannukah menorah has eight branches to represent the eight days that the little jar of oil lasted. In the centre is the servant candle from which the other eight are lit. The festival lasts for eight days. One candle is lit on the first night, two on the second and so on. (See cover picture.)

The picture above shows a Jewish family in the Yemen celebrating Hannukah.

This is a dreidl, a small spinning top that children play with at Hannukah. On each side is one of the letters N, G, H, S. These stand for Nes Gadol Haya Sham – 'a great miracle happened there'.

The Temple menorah had seven lights and it has become a symbol for the Jewish people. You can see it on flags, gravestones and in many synagogues.

The giant menorah in the picture below stands outside the Parliament building (the Knesset) in Jerusalem.

SUCCOT

(also known as Tabernacles)
This family is building a succah (a small hut) in their garden ready for the festival of Succot (plural of succah). They have cut down branches to make a roof and will hang fruit and flowers from it.

Succot is a thanksgiving for the harvest. It takes place in autumn, in the month of Tishri. It is also a reminder of how God took care of the Israelites after they had escaped from Egypt (see p. 22) and lived for 40 years in tents in the desert. Ever since then Jews have made succot to show that they must completely trust God to take care of them. Many families make their own succah and eat their meals in it as often as they can during the eight days of the festival.

A succah may also be built in the synagogue.
The worshippers carry palm branches, tied with myrtle and willow leaves (called lulav), and a kind of large lemon called an etrog. These symbols of the good things that grow are pointed in every direction to show that God's goodness is everywhere.

The picture on the right shows Jews praying at the Western Wall of the Temple at Succot.

palm
myrtle
willow
etrog

1. In the photograph at the top of the opposite page, what is the little boy doing?
2. What was the miracle that happened at the Temple?
3. Look at the photograph of the Hannukah menorah in the window. Why are only half the candles lit?
4. (a) What is a dreidl? (b) What do the letters N, G, H, S stand for?
5. In the picture at the top of this page, what is the family doing?
6. What do Jews remember at Succot?
7. In the picture taken at the Western Wall, what are the men and boys carrying?
8. Find six pictures in this book which show a menorah. Write down the numbers of the pages where you find them.
9. Draw pictures of: (a) a Temple menorah; (b) a Hannukah menorah; (c) a lulav; (d) an etrog.

14 More festivals

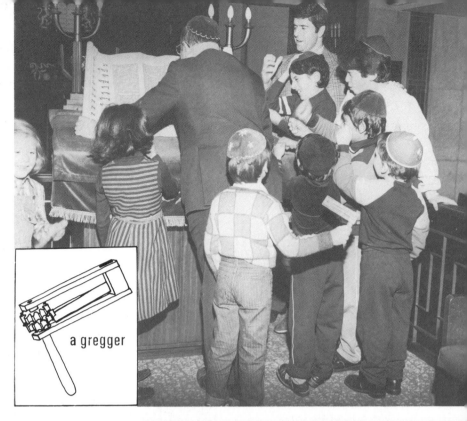

PURIM (also called the Feast of Lots)

Purim is a joyful festival: it celebrates the Bible story of Esther. The wicked Haman plotted to have all the Jews killed because he was angry with Mordecai. But Mordecai's cousin, Esther, Queen of Persia, risked her life to tell the King. So Haman himself was hung and the Jews were safe.

As the story of Esther is read out in the synagogue, children stamp their feet and rattle greggers every time they hear Haman's name.

The top picture on this page shows a rabbi reading the story of Esther to children in a synagogue in London.

It has become the custom to wear fancy dress and act in Purim plays. The middle photograph is of a Purim procession in Israel.

The picture on the right was taken at a nursery school in Manchester.

Special cakes are baked at Purim and people take presents to their friends.

a gregger

LAG B'OMER

The days between Pesah and Shavuot are solemn ones, recalling the suffering of the Jews under the Romans. No parties or weddings are held on these 'sefira' (counting) days, except for Lag B'Omer, which is a joyful day of bonfires and picnics. Stories are told about the great heroes of 2000 years ago – the much-loved Rabbi Akiba, the brave warrior Bar Kochba and the great scholar Bar Yohai.

Children shoot with bows and arrows (as Bar Kochba did). Candles are lit at the tomb of Bar Yohai in Israel.

TU B'SHVAT: the New Year for trees. Trees are very important in God's creation. They are mentioned often in the Bible. In recent years the planting of trees has helped to make Israel more fertile. Every year on Tu B'Shvat thousands of Jews in Israel plant trees. Jews in other countries collect money to send to Israel.

TISHA B'AV

On this day, the saddest in the year, both the first and the second Temples were destroyed. For twenty-four hours Jews fast. In the synagogue the men sit on the ground or on low stools, the curtain of the Ark is taken down and the lights are dim.

1. What did Queen Esther do?
2. What are the children doing in the synagogue in the picture opposite?
3. Look at the masks on the wall in the bottom picture opposite. Whose faces do they show?
4. Why are the days between Pesah and Shavuot so solemn?
5. What is different about Lag B'Omer at this time?
6. Why is the woman above lighting a candle? Where is she?
7. Why are the men sitting on the ground in the picture above?
8. Write down all the activities you can see children doing in the photographs on these two pages. Draw three of them.

TORAH AND TRADITION

The first chapter in this book is called 'Torah'. Prayer and the study of the Torah are very important to Jews. This book will end by explaining the importance of Tradition. For Jews tradition means the customs, the festivals and the wisdom which have grown up around the keeping of God's laws. These have been passed on by parents to their children through the ages. Tradition has kept the Jewish faith strong in times of trouble and it links Jews together even when they are far apart. There is a lot about festivals in this book; festivals are an important way to keep traditions going, especially as much of the festival activity takes place in the home. Here are some words of a song from a famous musical play called *Fiddler on the Roof*. It is about a poor Jewish family in the U.S.S.R.

How do we keep our balance?
That I can tell you in one word.
TRADITION!
Because of our traditions we have kept our balance for many years.
Here in Anatevka we have our traditions for everything: how to sleep, how to eat, how to work, even how to wear our clothes.

For instance, we always keep our heads covered and we wear these little prayer shawls.
This shows our constant devotion (love) to God.
You may ask, 'How did this tradition get started?'
I'll tell you: I don't know.
But it's a Tradition.
Because of our Traditions everyone here knows who he is and what God expects him to do.
Without our Traditions our life would be as shaky ... as shaky ... as a fiddler on the roof!

Listen to the record or tape or, even better, see the film or a stage production.

Write about some of the traditions your own family keeps. If you are Jewish, write down some more of the traditions you keep at festival times.

Find eight pictures in this book which show the importance of Torah to Jews and write about them.

Find eight pictures in this book which show traditions being followed and write about them.

Below is a picture of a family sitting down to an evening meal. How can you tell they are Jewish? Make a list of at least 12 clues.

Look at the drawings on the opposite page. They are all part of the traditions of special events. Copy and colour them and write down which festival or event each one belongs to.

Tasks

Note   Try to work in small groups for some of these tasks.

CHAPTER 1   Make a miniature Torah scroll with two sticks or kitchen rolls, paper, glue, velvet for a cover, milk-bottle tops, silver thread, Hebrew writing.

CHAPTER 2   Try to listen to or read these songs and write down the words: 'Go down Moses', 'By the Rivers of Babylon' and 'Exodus'. Why do you think black people in America and Britain sing these songs from Jewish history?

CHAPTER 3   Find out from library books more about the history of Jews living in Britain. Lincoln, London, York, Manchester and Oxford are key places.

CHAPTER 4   Ask for leaflets about Israel at a travel agent. Cut out some of the pictures to make an interesting collage. Draw the Israeli flag.

CHAPTER 5   Try to visit a synagogue. If that is not possible, make a model of the inside of a synagogue out of clay, papier mâché or cardboard boxes.

CHAPTER 6   Find out about a local Jewish organization *or* find out more about the JWB. Their address is: P. & A. Dept, 221 Golders Green Road, London W11. Display your findings.

CHAPTER 7   Do some study yourself: find out from the Bible and other books about one of the great heroes mentioned on p. 14. Write a short account. *Or* find out and write a few lines about each of the famous Jews illustrated on p.14.

CHAPTER 8   Write a story, imagining you are visiting a Jewish home for the first time. What happens? What do you see? Is there anything that surprises you? Try to buy something with a kosher label on it from a large supermarket.

CHAPTER 9   Make some hallah bread *or* try to spend a peaceful day without using anything that would cause another person to work that day!

CHAPTER 10   Make a model of a huppah. Use peg or wire figures for the bride, bridegroom and the rabbi with the ketubah. Dress them with scrap materials.

CHAPTER 11   Make a seder dish out of clay or plasticine *or* write and act out a play based on the Bible story of Pesah.

CHAPTER 12   Copy on to card the Jewish year diagram on p. 25. Fix a big cardboard arrow in the middle with a . Point it to the present month and move it round as the weeks go by.

CHAPTER 13   Make a dreidl from wood or cardboard. Paint one of the letters nun, gimel, hay and shin on each side (see p. 14). Play a spinning game for nuts or sweets.

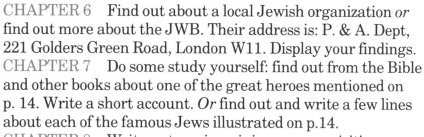

CHAPTER 14   Read the Book of Esther in the Bible. Make masks for the main characters and write or act a play of the story. (The audience could make greggers or noisy rattles to shake every time Haman appears!)

Try to read *The Power of Light: Eight Stories for Hannukah* by Isaac Bashevis Singer (Robson Books).

31

NOTES FOR TEACHERS

This book is intended for use with 9–14 year olds. No previous knowledge of Judaism or of religious terminology is assumed. Essential aspects of history and denomination are covered only in so far as they explain Jewish belief and practice today. The text is deliberately simple in vocabulary and presentation. Most of the questions at the end of each chapter can be answered with a single sentence, but are designed to elicit fuller answers from the more able. The Bible references given throughout the text are the same as those in the Christian 'Old Testament'.

It is suggested that before using this book a general introduction to Judaism be given to the whole class. Ideally this should be done by using: a filmstrip; a recording of part of a synagogue service; recordings of Hebrew songs; Jewish artifacts, e.g. tallit, kippah, menorah, Shabbat candlesticks, lulav, dreidl, seder dish. Thereafter, the chapters need not be used in order. Pupils might work on different chapters of their own choosing. (Some libraries and local R.E. resource centres are able to lend artifacts.) The book mentioned at the foot of p. 31 is highly recommended.

It would be of great value, while this book is being studied, to arrange a visit to a synagogue and to encourage pupils to talk to Jews about their religion. The optional Tasks list contains ideas for research outside the classroom, perhaps in small groups. The work is obviously dependent to some extent on the location of the school and the facilities available.

The Jewish National Fund (J.N.F.) Youth and Education Office has a wide range of useful teaching material. Particularly recommended is the book 'Craft in action throughout the Jewish Year' by Helen Miller and Judith Rabin. It has excellent ideas for making simple games, artifacts, decorations, etc. Catalogue from J.N.F., Harold Poster House, Kingsbury Circle, London NW9 9SP. The CEM Video *Judaism through the eyes of Jewish children* is recommended as an introduction to the religion. It is available on VHS or Betamax.

ACKNOWLEDGEMENTS

The author wishes to thank Rabbi Norman Solomon, Rabbi Julia Neuberger, Clive Lawton, Stuart Pollock and Shula Engel-Davis for their help and critical advice.

Thanks are also due to the following for the use of their photographs. Auschwitz Museum, Poland: p. 6 (Auschwitz); BBC: p. 6 (Young); BBC Hulton Picture Library: p. 14 (Maimonides, Mendelssohn, Rothschild); BIPAC: pp. 2 (Simhat Torah), 5 (both), 10 (synagogue exterior), 13 (prayer), 20 (circumcision), 23, 24 (shofar, beach), 26 (Yemen, Knesset), 27 (Western Wall), 28 procession, 29 (shrine, tree-planting, Tisha B'av); Camera Press; pp. 9 (soldiers, Arab and Jew), 29 (archery); John Child: p. 13 (Hannukah); Peter Fisher: p. 15 (rabbis visiting); Judy Goldhill: pp. 15 (tefillin), 28 (nursery school); Jewish Chronicle: pp. 2 (scroll), 3 (all), 6 (Menuhin, notice-board), 7 (street party), 10 (Progressive synagogue), 18 (hallah), 21 (funeral), 22; J.N.F.: p. 8 (pumping station); JWB: p. 13 (marathon, elderly man); Gemma Levine: pp. 9 (kibbutz), 15 (yeshiva), 19, 20 (marriage); Marks & Spencer: p. 6 (penny bazaar); MEPhA: pp. 4, 8 (street sign); Photo Source: p. 8 (Jerusalem); Ronald Sheridan's Photo-Library: p. 12 (Sinai); Juliette Soester: pp. 10 (Orthodox synagogue), 11 (ladies' guild), 18 (Shabbat meal), 21 (bar mitzvah, cemetery), 28 (synagogue). Weidenfeld Archives: p. 14 (Einstein). The remaining photographs are by the author.

The line drawing on p. 30 is by Peter Kesteven.

The extracts from the pocket diary on pp. 19 and 25 are by permission of the J.N.F. and the diagram on p. 25 is adapted from their poster. The words from *Fiddler on the Roof* on p. 30 are used by permission of Carlin Music Corporation, 14 New Burlington Street, London, and Chappell & Intersong Music Group Australia Ltd.

Cover pictures: (inner photograph) family celebrating Hannukah (Yael Braun, Camera Press); (outer photograph) Western Wall, Jerusalem (J. Messerschmidt, Camera Press).

Answers to quiz on p. 30:
mezuzah, tallit, Shabbat candles, hallah, picture of Jerusalem, menorah, kippahs, book with Hebrew writing, dreidl, book about Israel, Bar Mitzvah card, Israeli flag.

The symbols on p. 31 are:
(left, from the top)
lulav, etrog (Succot)
shofar (Rosh Hashanah)
matzot (Pesah)
gregger (Purim)
Havdallah candle
dreidl (Hannukah)
(right, from the top)
Hannukah menorah
bow and arrow (Lag B'Omer)
Jahrzeit candle (death)
hallah (Shabbat)
judgement scales (Yom Kippur)
huppah (marriage)

RELIGIOUS AND MORAL
EDUCATION PRESS
A Member of the Pergamon Group of Companies

Copyright © 1986 Sarah Thorley
All Rights Reserved
ISBN 0 08-031778-2 non net
ISBN 0 08-031779-0 net
Printed in Great Britain by
A. Wheaton & Co. Ltd, Exeter